INSIDE MAGIC

STUNTS, PUZZLES, AND STAGE ILLUSIONS

Nicholas Einhorn

New York

This edition published in 2011 by:

The Rosen Publishing Group, Inc.
29 East 21st Street, New York, NY 10010

Library of Congress Cataloging-in-Publication Data

Einhorn, Nicholas.
Stunts, puzzles, and stage illusions / Nicholas Einhorn.
        p. cm. — (Inside magic)
Includes bibliographical references and index.
ISBN 978-1-4358-9454-9 (library binding)
1. Magic tricks—Juvenile literature. I. Title.
GV1548.E335 2011
793.8—dc22

                                                                                2010010093

Manufactured in the United States of America

CPSIA Compliance Information: Batch #S10YA: For further information, contact Rosen Publishing, New York, New York, at 1-800-237-9932.

Copyright in design, text and images © 2007, 2009 Anness Publishing Limited, U.K. Previously published as part of a larger volume: *Magical Illusions, Conjuring Tricks, Amazing Puzzles & Stunning Stunts.*

Photography by Paul Bricknell © Anness

CONTENTS

INTRODUCTION

A stunt is a feat displaying unusual strength, skill, or daring. These can range in scale from the very small to the very large. One of the most famous magicians known for his large-scale stunts was none other than the great showman Harry Houdini (1874–1926). In order to promote his forthcoming shows at theaters across the world, he would often challenge the local police to lock him up in their apparently "escape-proof" handcuffs. He would then generate immense publicity by promptly escaping from them.

In recent years, the American showman David Blaine has resurrected the genre of publicity stunts. In one of his latest enterprises, in 2003, he starved himself for forty-four days, sealed inside a 7 x 7 x 3 ft (2 x 2 x 1 m) transparent box suspended over London's Tower Bridge, and in New York, in 2006, he unsuccessfully attempted to spend a week submerged in a water-filled sphere. These dangerous stunts have earned him millions of dollars and worldwide fame. The stunts you will learn in this book are unlikely to earn you millions or make you famous and are a little more modest than Houdini's or Blaine's. However, they are still a lot of fun to perform and for your friends to witness.

This book will also enable you to set up challenges for your friends to solve. These puzzles test people's ability to look at a situation from many angles and to use problem-solving techniques to find the solutions.

Finally, this book explains how to construct and perform some amazing stage illusions. "Illusion" is the term used to describe big, choreographed tricks. Cutting an assistant in half or making him or her appear to levitate are both good examples. Although this category of magic can be an expensive one to specialize in, it need not cost you much to make a few illusions for yourself. In this book, you will discover the secrets of several basic tricks that look impressive when performed with confidence.

Follow the Leader

No matter how closely people follow your movements, they are unlikely to be able to replicate what you do here. While you will succeed every time, most of your audience will start off with their fingers in the wrong position and will therefore fail to replicate your actions.

1. Tell everyone to copy every move you make. Cross your arms in front of you, hold your hands palm to palm, and interlock your fingers. The key to this trick is to make sure that the right arm goes over the left and the right little finger is on top.

2. Now bring your hands in to your chest and up toward your face. Stick out your index fingers.

3. Explain to the audience that you must use the back of the index finger of each hand to touch either side of your nose. This is awkward, but entirely possible.

4. Finally, without taking your fingers off your nose, you untwist your fingers and open your arms to reach the position shown.

◆ ◆ ◆ ◆ ◆ ◆ ◆ ◆

Still Following the Leader

Again, tell everyone to copy every move you make. Hold your hands out in front of you, palm to palm, and interlock your fingers. As the others copy you, unlock your fingers and comment that the right arm should be over the left (use your hands to gesture as you speak, to justify taking your hands apart). This excuse enables you to reposition your arms as follows.

1. When you interlock your fingers again, twist your left hand counter-clockwise instead of clockwise, so that when your hands come together, although it looks as if your arms are crossed as they were before, they aren't really.

2. Tell the spectators to follow your movements. Slowly give your hands a quarter turn clockwise, bringing you to the position shown. Everyone else will be mixed up and won't be able to replicate your simple move.

TIP

If you find it difficult to get into the position in step 1, simply lock your hands together as in step 2 and twist your hands counter-clockwise until you can't turn them anymore. This is the position you need to get into.

Hypnotic, Magnetic Fingers

You apparently hypnotize your subjects as you demonstrate how the power of the mind can cause the body to do things against its will, making the volunteer's fingers close together involuntarily. Although this stunt is not really hypnosis, some stage hypnotists do try it out on an audience before a show in order to see how susceptible people are to the power of suggestion.

1. Ask the spectators to interlock their fingers and hold their index fingers out in front of them. They must separate their fingertips as much as possible. Explain that you are going to hypnotize them, and tell them a story about very strong magnets being implanted in the tips of their fingers, drawing their fingertips closer together until they lock together. You can also mime binding people's fingers together with invisible thread.

2. Believe it or not, the spectators will find they can do nothing to resist their fingers getting closer together until they touch. Why does this work? The fingers are being stretched apart at the beginning, and after a few moments muscle fatigue sets in and the muscles have to contract.

Wand Twist

The challenge is to copy the magician with a simple move that seems easy to replicate. However, unless they know the secret, few will be able to succeed. Make it clear at the beginning that they are not allowed to let go of the wand or stick at any time.

1. With your hands held palm to palm, hold a magic wand, pencil or other stick-like object with your thumbs as shown.

2. Cross your thumbs, right over left. This will make the wand start to twist to the right.

3. The right hand turns downward and the left upward, palms wiping against each other. The stick remains between the thumbs.

4. Continue turning the hands until the palms are facing the floor. When these moves are all put together, the crossing of the thumbs goes unnoticed. People will get themselves into a mess, ending up with their hands pointing in opposite directions.

Floating Arms

This weird stunt is something I used to do all the time as a teenager. It is very effective and creates a really strange sensation. As with many of the stunts in this chapter, you have to try it yourself in order to realize how odd the experience is.

1. Stand behind someone and hold her arms to her sides. She must push her arms outward for about 45 seconds.

2. When you let go, the other person's arms will rise upward as if they are being pulled up by invisible strings.

Pepper-sepper-ation

A small quantity of pepper is sprinkled onto the surface of a glass of water. The magician touches the water with the tip of a toothpick, and the pepper reacts by moving away from the toothpick in the most dramatic way. When anyone else tries to copy the stunt, it won't work.

Secret View

1. Coat the tip of a toothpick with a dot of liquid soap.

2. Sprinkle some pepper into a glass of water.

3. There should be enough pepper to cover the surface. Now touch the tip of the toothpick to the center of the surface of the water.

4. Watch as the pepper jumps away from the toothpick. Remove the toothpick from the water and wipe the end dry, removing all traces of soap as you do so. When someone else tries the trick, either with the same or a different toothpick, it won't work.

TIP

Use a pen instead of a toothpick. If you keep a tiny piece of sponge soaked in liquid soap in the cap of the pen, it will be ready to work at any moment. In fact, when you put the lid on the pen to put it away, it will recoat itself for your next performance.

Table Lock

If you really want to make a friend look silly, try this the next time you are together. Be prepared to make a quick exit!

Ask your friend to place both hands palm down, flat on the table. Now take two full glasses, and carefully balance them on the backs of your friend's hands. She will now be unable to move her hands without the glasses falling and the drinks spilling everywhere. This is a good time for you and your other friends to walk away and leave your victim sitting alone in this awkward predicament!

=TIP=

It is not advisable to perform this stunt on a surface that could be damaged by the spilled drinks.

Broom Suspension

This trick leaves your victim high, but not necessarily dry. Only try it in suitable surroundings and never without the permission of the person who lives there. It is especially funny when you trick somebody who is a bit of a know-all or show-off.

1. You will need a plastic cup (it must be plastic, never glass) full of water and a long stick. A broom handle is perfect, but a pool cue might also do the job. Stand your victim up, and ask him or her to hold the stick in the air. Now climb on a chair and trap the plastic cup between the end of the stick and the ceiling.

2. That's all there is to it: You can just walk away or continue your conversation some distance away. Your victim will be stuck wondering how to move without getting soaked. If the person finds a way to do it, let me know!

Time for a Shower

This party challenge could result in someone getting very wet, so you should only attempt it in an area that can easily be cleaned and won't be damaged by liquid being spilled. You may have to practice the stunt a few times before you get it right.

1. Place a plate over a glass full of liquid. Here we have used colored liquid so you can see what is happening.

2. Hold the glass firmly to the plate and turn everything over. Put it back on the table. The challenge is to drink the liquid inside the glass, but you are allowed to use only one hand.

3. The secret to achieving this is to hold the plate and push your forehead firmly against the base of the glass.

4. Now slowly and carefully stand upright. Make sure the glass is balanced properly.

5. Once the glass is vertical and balanced, remove the plate.

6. Now you can put the plate down and lift the glass from your forehead, leaving you in a position to drink the liquid normally.

Coin Through Hole

The challenge is to push a large coin through a hole only half its size. The paper can be folded but not torn. Allow spectators to try doing it themselves before you show them how it is done. Unless they have seen the stunt before, they won't be able to do it.

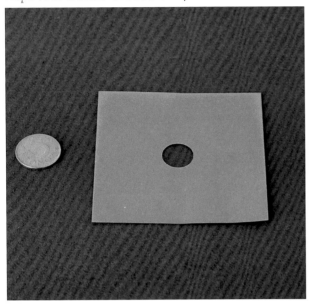

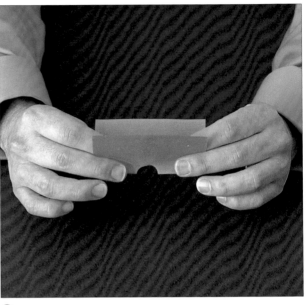

1. Carefully cut a hole about ⅝ in (1.5 cm) in diameter in a piece of paper. You will also need a coin that is clearly larger than the hole.

2. Fold the piece of paper in half, with the hole facing down, toward the table.

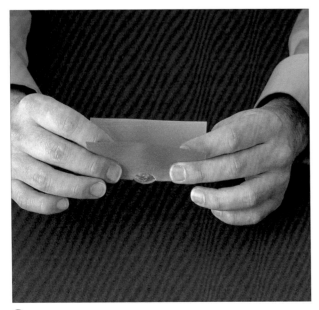

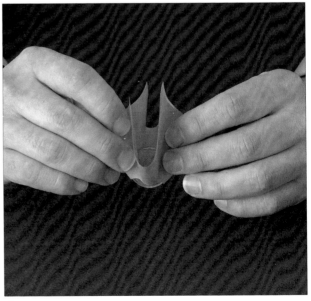

3. Drop the coin into the folded piece of paper so that it rests in the hole.

4. Now bend the paper upward as shown. This action will stretch the hole.

5. This allows you to push the coin carefully through the hole without damaging the paper.

6. You may need to experiment with holes and coins of different sizes in order to create the best-looking illusion possible.

Rising Tube Mystery

A paper tube held together with paper clips is seen threaded onto two lengths of cord. Defying gravity, the tube not only remains suspended when held upright, but rises up the cords in an uncanny fashion. Everything is handed out for examination.

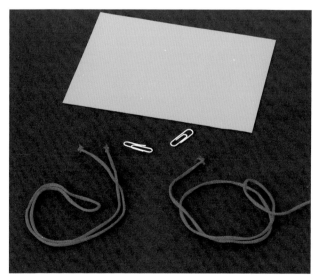

1. You will need a sheet of paper, two paper clips and two identical, long pieces of cord.

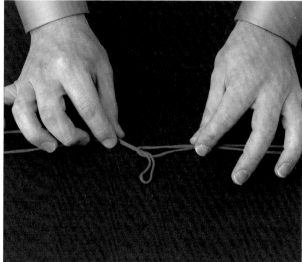

2. Fold both lengths of cord in half, and insert the center of one through the other to create a small loop.

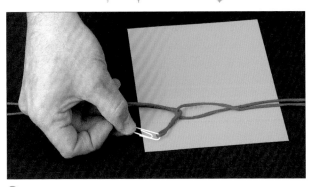

3. Attach a paper clip to the loop, and clip this onto the edge of the paper.

4. If you have attached it properly, the setup should now look like this, and everything should be secure.

5. Now roll up the paper into a tight tube so that the cord is on the inside.

6. Once the whole sheet is rolled, reposition the paper clip so that it holds the roll together.

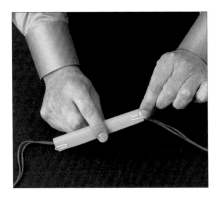

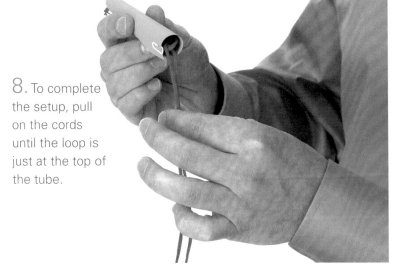

8. To complete the setup, pull on the cords until the loop is just at the top of the tube.

7. Use a second paper clip to hold the roll securely at the other end. This one should be clipped only to the paper and not to the cords.

9. Hold the cords up by the end, and show that the tube is defying gravity.

10. Grip the bottom cords and pull very gently.

11. The tube will slowly travel up the cords!

12. When the tube reaches the top, hold both ends of the cords together, and begin to disassemble the cords from the paper.

13. Remove both paper clips, and show them to the audience.

14. Unroll the paper, and hand everything out to the audience for examination. You can even challenge them to try to do it themselves!

Suspended Animation

A mug dropped from a height is expected to hit the floor and shatter, but instead it stops short and remains suspended in the air. As with many stunts, science plays a key role, enabling you to harness the laws of physics and perform an extraordinary feat.

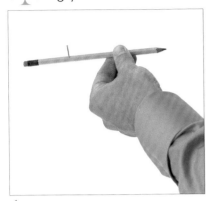

1. Prepare by tapping a nail into the side of a pencil.

2. Tie one end of a long piece of cord to the handle of a mug and the other end to a washer.

3. Hold the washer in one hand and the pencil in the other. The cord hangs over the pencil.

4. This close-up view shows how the string sits alongside the nail.

5. The cord is released, and the mug plunges toward the floor.

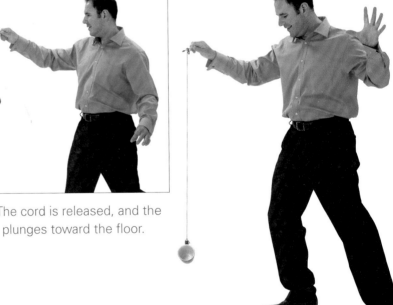

6. Amazingly, the cord winds itself around the pencil, stopping the mug from hitting the floor and breaking.

7. This close-up view shows how the weight of the washer stops the cord from unwinding and the nail helps to stop the cord from slipping.

Straw Bottle

The challenge is to pick up a bottle with a straw. There are several ways you can achieve this, including tying the straw around the neck of the bottle, but the solution shown below is more fun and less obvious and, therefore, more impressive.

1. Display a bottle, and challenge the spectators to lift it from the table using just a drinking straw.

2. The solution is simple. Bend the straw about one-third of the way up, and then insert it into the bottle. The fold in the straw will spring open inside, and it will lock into place, enabling you to lift the bottle off the table.

Immovable

As a demonstration of your superhuman strength, you touch your index fingers together at the tips and challenge someone to pull them apart. Nobody can do it! You can combine this trick with Try to Stand Up! as they work nicely together.

Touch your fingertips together, holding your arms as shown. As long as your opponent holds your wrists, she will fail to move your fingertips apart. The person's energy is dissipated, leaving your fingers unaffected.

TIP
These stunts look especially impressive when the challenger is a child or someone who is smaller and clearly weaker than the person he or she is challenging.

Card Flick

Have you ever seen a tablecloth whipped off a table, leaving all the glasses and cutlery in place? This is a scaled-down version. It is considerably easier to achieve after a little practice, although no less impressive than the larger scale version.

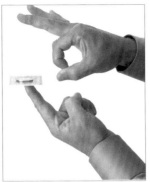

1. Begin by balancing a coin on top of a playing card on the tip of your finger.

2. Get ready to flick the card away from you.

3. If you are quick, the card will shoot out from under the coin, leaving it neatly on the tip of your finger.

The Rice Lift

How do you lift a jar of uncooked rice with a single chopstick? You can also use a pencil or knife in place of the chopstick. Other types of containers can be used, but the important factor is the shape: The container must have a "shoulder" below the neck.

3. When you can physically feel the resistance, give the chopstick one last push all the way down to the bottom of the jar and then lift the jar slowly from the table.

1. Fill a jar with short grain, uncooked rice. Put the lid on the jar, and bang on the table to pack the rice down as far as possible. Remove the lid, and push the chopstick down into the rice.

2. Work the chopstick up and down 30–50 times. This motion will pack the rice tightly against the sides of the jar. The more you "stab" the rice, the harder it will become to pull the chopstick free.

Try to Stand Up!

You prove you arc incredibly strong by stopping someone from standing up using just one finger. This effective trick is particularly funny when a child pins a parent or other adult to the chair, and it can easily be incorporated into any show.

Ask someone to sit down on a chair, and hold your first finger against her forehead. Tell her she is not allowed to remove your finger. She now has to try to stand up. She won't be able to do it because her center of balance is above her lap, and she can't move her head forward to compensate for that.

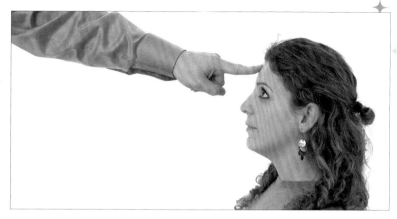

Surefire Bet

Ask someone to stand with her back to the wall. You place a large denomination bill in front of her feet, and explain that she can keep the note if she can pick it up without losing contact with the wall. She will be unable to do it, and you will keep the money.

1. When you position the person, make sure her heels are touching the wall. Explain that her heels must not lose contact with the wall. Place the bill just in front of her feet.

2. She will be unable to pick up the bill without losing her balance. Shifting her center of gravity causes her to fall away from the wall, and there is nothing she can do about it.

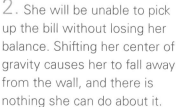

Lift Me If You Can

How is it possible to drain someone of his strength in a split second? Easy, just read on! It is even more impressive if you train a small child to do this stunt so that he can confuse an adult.

1. Stand with your arms folded up and your elbows locked in to your sides.

2. Get someone to lift you off the ground holding you by your elbows. In this position, it is relatively easy.

3. When you want to create the illusion of making the person seem instantly weak, simply move your elbows out to the position shown. It is a subtle difference, but one that really matters.

4. Now it is impossible for him to raise you off the ground at all, because moving the elbows out has shifted the center of gravity.

Superman

In yet another demonstration of your superhuman strength, you hold a broomstick or a pole in both hands and challenge anyone to push you off your spot. Nobody, no matter how big and strong he or she is, will be able to do it.

1. Hold a broom handle or other long stick with both hands, and make sure that your feet are shoulder-width apart and your elbows are bent. Your challenger takes hold of the broom with both hands outside yours. Try as she might, she cannot push you off the spot.

2. This stunt also works if you hold the ends of the broom and she places her hands in the middle. Bending your arms simply dissipates all the energy that is being thrown at you.

Coin Con

In this stunt, you have to remove the paper the coins are resting on, but leave the coins in place balanced on the rims of the glasses. This stunt uses the same method as that which was used for Card Flick. It may require a few tries in order for it to work properly.

1. Place two coins on a slip of paper resting on two glasses.

2. Simply strike the paper firmly with your finger, in the center and straight down to the table. The speed of the movement will free the paper and leave both coins sitting on the edge of the glasses, undisturbed.

Riddle Me This

Ask your friends this riddle, and see if they can work out which card is where. This simple conundrum is particularly good when you pose it at a party or other social occasion where a group of people may not know each other, as it will get people talking.

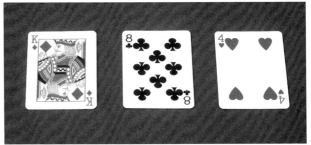

1. The riddle is:
"To the left of a club is a king.
To the right of a king is an eight.
The diamond is not the four or next to the four.
Home is where the heart is."

2. And here is the answer. Did you get it right? Now try challenging friends and family to solve it.

Letter of Resignation

Can you draw the design in step 5 without taking your pen off the paper and without going over any line twice? Even though there are only a limited number of ways this can be attempted, it is surprising how long it takes to work it out.

1. Start at the bottom right corner and smoothly draw the shape shown.

2. Continue to draw, as shown, making sure the pen doesn't leave the paper.

3. Complete the outside of the shape as shown in the picture.

4. Finally, complete the x in the middle of the box. Practice a few times before you try to challenge anyone else to do it.

5. When you try this out on someone else, you will need to show him a picture of the final design, so make sure that you have one to hand out before you begin.

Bullseye

Or try this puzzle: Can you draw a dot in the center of a circle without taking your pen off the paper? This is possible, but only if you cheat a little, which will both infuriate and amuse the people whom you challenge to solve the puzzle.

1. Loosely fold over the top corner of a piece of paper. Make a dot where the corner meets the page.

2. Now run the pen across the folded corner and back onto the front of the sheet.

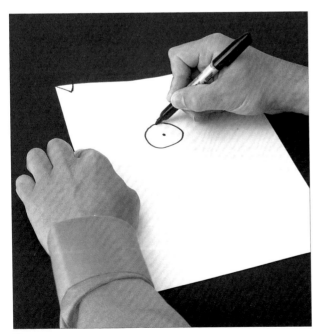

3. Allow the paper to unfold, and draw the circle around the central dot.

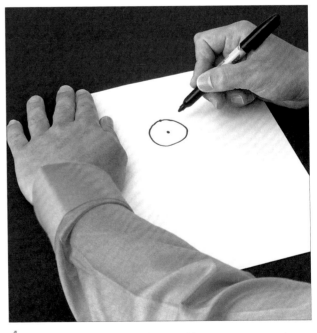

4. This completes the picture. You are now ready to challenge someone to try to do it.

Total This Sum

This is the perfect puzzle to show a math teacher or accountant. Try it yourself, and see how deceptive it is. Simply add up the numbers listed below. If you get a total of 5,000 then you are wrong, and you will need to try again.

Write down the following numbers:
1,000; 40; 1,000; 30; 1,000; 20; 1,000; 10.
Add them up, and see what total you get.

=TIP=

People get a total of 5,000 because they begin to count in a rhythm that makes them incorrectly anticipate what the answer is.

Impossible Numbers!

Write down the following number on a piece of paper as quickly as possible: eleven thousand, eleven hundred, and eleven. Tricky, isn't it? Now ask your friends and family to try it – you will be amazed how few people get it right the first time.

1. Did you write down 11,1111? If so, then you are incorrect and should try again.

2. This number is so difficult to write because of the way it is said. "Eleven hundred" is, of course, one thousand, one hundred, but most people write a string of ones in an attempt to write it as quickly as possible.

Calculation Sensation

Someone thinks of any number between 1 and 63. With the aid of six cards (each with a huge list of numbers on it) the magician can reveal what the number was that the spectator thought of. It is one of the oldest mathematical puzzles, and it is still very effective.

1. Use a computer to make the six cards you will use for the calculation. These are the numbers you should type on each:

Card 1: 1 3 5 7 9 11 13 15 17 19 21 23 25 27 29 31 33 35 37 39 41 43 45 47 49 51 53 55 57 59 61

Card 2: 2 3 6 7 10 11 14 15 18 19 22 23 26 27 30 31 34 35 38 39 42 43 46 47 50 51 54 55 58 59 62 63

Card 3: 4 5 6 7 12 13 14 15 20 21 22 23 28 29 30 31 36 37 38 39 44 45 46 47 52 53 54 55 60 61 62 63

Card 4: 8 9 10 11 12 13 14 15 24 25 26 27 28 29 30 31 40 41 42 43 44 45 46 47 56 57 58 59 60 61 62 63

Card 5: 16 17 18 19 20 21 22 23 24 25 26 27 28 29 30 31 48 49 50 51 52 53 54 55 56 57 58 59 60 61 62 63

Card 6: 32 33 34 35 36 37 38 39 40 41 42 43 44 45 46 47 48 49 50 51 52 53 54 55 56 57 58 59 60 61 62 63

As long as you keep these groups of numbers together, you can make cards of any shape you like. Just make sure the first number is always top left.

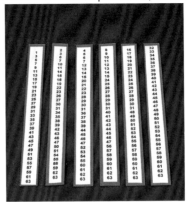

2. Ask a volunteer to think of a number between 1 and 63. Show him the cards in any order, and ask him to tell you if his number appears on it. If it does, remember the top number. Continue showing the cards, asking the same question each time. Each time he say "yes," add the number at the top of the card, keeping a running total in your head.

3. After all the cards have been seen, the total in your head is the number that the person is thinking of. In this example, that number is 37.

Hide and Seek

While your back is turned, an object is placed under one of three mugs. When you turn around, you are able to pick the correct mug every single time. This trick requires a stooge or confederate, whom no one will suspect. You must be sure not to glance at your helper in an obvious way. The trick will keep spectators baffled for a long time, as long as you are both subtle.

2. Your confederate watches carefully and indicates the correct mug by holding up the relevant number of fingers. In this example, the object is under the third mug.

1. Place three mugs upside down in a row on the table. Turn your back, and ask someone to place a small object under any of the mugs. Then turn around.

Hide and Seek Solo

While your back is turned, an object is placed under one of three mugs and the position of the two empty mugs is switched. When you turn around, you know where the object is. You can repeat this trick again and again. It will fool even the brightest people.

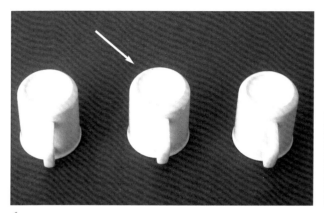

1. You will need three opaque cups or mugs, one of which must have an identifying feature on its base. Any tiny mark or blemish that you will recognize will work. Put the three mugs upside down in a row, with the marked mug in the center.

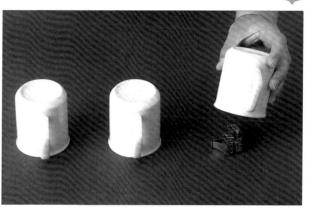

2. Turn your back and instruct someone to place an object such as a coin or watch under any mug.

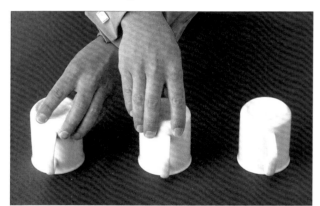

3. Tell the volunteer to switch the positions of the two empty mugs while your back is turned.

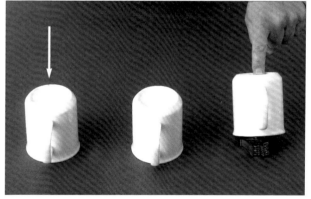

4. When you turn around, look for the marked mug. If it is still in the middle, that is where the object must be. If the marked mug is now at one end of the row, the object will be under the cup at the opposite end.

TIP

You may find that borrowed mugs already have small identifying features, such as chips or scratches, if you look closely enough. If you want to use your own cups, it is easy to mark one of them, but be sure to make it subtle.

Topsy-Turvy Mugs

In this classic puzzle, you line up three mugs with one upside down. Then by turning two mugs at a time, you manage to get all three the right way up in just three moves. When you challenge others to do the same, they just won't be able to do it. Why not? Because you cheat!

1. Line up three mugs, placing the mug at each end mouth down and the center mug mouth up. This is the starting position for the puzzle.

2. Pick up the left-hand mug and the center mug. In one swift movement, turn both mugs over and place them back where they were. This is move 1.

3. Now pick up the end mugs. Once again, turn them both over and put them back where they came from. This is move 2.

4. Finally, turn over the left hand mug and the center mug (repeating move 1). This third and final move will result in all three mugs being mouth up.

5. Turn over the center mug, and challenge a spectator to do what you just did. Here is the sneaky part: The mugs are in fact now laid out in the exact opposite way to the way they were when you did it. The spectators won't notice this small change and will be baffled as to how you managed to get all three mugs facing up in just three moves.

X-ray Vision

While your back is turned, a coin is placed under a mug. When you turn around, you are able to determine what denomination of coin it is. This trick also requires a stooge or confederate, which means that you must teach it to a friend, who will be your secret helper when you perform it. The two of you need to practice the trick a lot so that you can get it right every time.

1. The handle of the mug can be turned to point in any direction. Take one coin of each denomination used in your currency, and lay them out around the mug like a clock. Put the lowest denomination at the 1 o'clock position, with the others equally spaced. This photograph shows British currency, which has eight different coins.

2. In performance you ask someone to place any coin on the table while your back is turned. Then you ask for the coin to be covered with the mug. This is when your friend picks up the mug and positions it so that the handle points in the correct direction for that coin. If you both always assume that the 12 o'clock position is where your friend is standing, you will always get the orientation of the mug correct. Which coin do you think is under the mug in this example?

3. Reveal the coin. Did you get it right?

Penny Pincher

The challenge is to remove both coins balanced on a glass at the same time, with one hand and without making direct contact with the glass. This may require some practice, but you will soon be able to perform it perfectly every time.

1. Balance two coins on the rim of a glass, arranging them on opposite sides, as shown here.

2. Place the tip of your thumb on one coin and the tip of your forefinger on the other coin.

3. Drag the coins onto the outside of the glass, being careful not to touch the glass with your hand or fingers.

4. Now raise your hand quickly, pinching your finger and thumb together. The coins will momentarily stick to your fingertips, and you can remove both coins together.

Invisible Traveler

In this deceptive puzzle, you cause a single card to travel from one place to another while everything is in the spectator's hands. This is also known as the Piano Trick. With a bit of thought, you can replace the playing cards with other objects that could make a fun presentation.

1. Begin with a deck of cards positioned in front of you. Ask a volunteer to place her hands flat on the table, palms down, as shown.

2. Pick up two cards from the top of the pile and say, "Two cards are even."

3. Place this pair between the pinky and ring fingers of the person's right hand. Now pick up two more cards and say again, "Two cards are even." Place these between the ring and middle fingers of the right hand.

4. Repeat this again and again on both hands until you reach the final space that is left between the left hand's ring and pinky fingers, where you place only one card and say: "One card is odd."

5. Pick up the first pair you dealt and split them, starting two piles on the table. As you lay the pair of cards down on the table say: "Even."

6. Repeat this dealing process, taking each pair and saying "even" as you lay the cards on the piles, until you have a single card remaining. Ask the person which pile she would like the odd card to be placed on. Put the last card down on the pile she points to.

7. Make a mystic pass over the two piles, and explain that you are invisibly transferring the odd card from one pile to the other. You now count out the piles, and it is seen that the pile containing an odd number of cards is the opposite pile to the one chosen for the odd card to be placed on! Really, nothing has happened. The fact is, before the single card was added to a pile in step 6, both piles contained an odd number of cards: because you split the pairs into two piles of seven cards. Your patter has created the impression that both piles are even, and that is what makes the trick work.

The Trapdoor Card

This superb puzzle is the brainchild of Robert Neale. There have been many versions of this trick over the years. I use a version in my professional work, as it is absolutely baffling and one of the very best puzzles you can learn. Do not underestimate the effect it will have on spectators. Thanks to Robert for allowing me to share his idea with you.

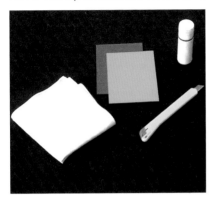

1. You will need some adhesive glue, a handkerchief, a craft knife and two pieces of card stock approximately 5 x 3 in (12.5 x 7.5 cm) in different colors (we used green and red in this example).

2. Glue the colored cards together back to back; then cut a trapdoor in the card. You should cut three sides, leaving one of the short ends intact for the hinge. The border should be about ¾ in (2 cm) wide. Crease the hinge sharply.

3. With the red side upward, ask someone to hold on to the trapdoor. Notice that the opening is facing away from the person.

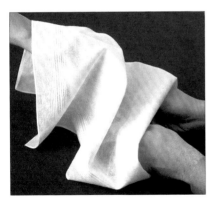

4. Explain that you are going to turn the card over, even though she will not let go of the card or turn her hand over. It doesn't sound possible. To keep the secret, throw a handkerchief over her hand and the card.

Secret View

5. The handkerchief has been removed in these pictures so you can see what is happening, but you must leave it in position while you make these moves. First, bend the end of the card underneath.

Secret View

6. Now roll the top underneath so that the folds overlap.

Secret View

7. Roll the sides of the card back, and bring them through the hole in the middle.

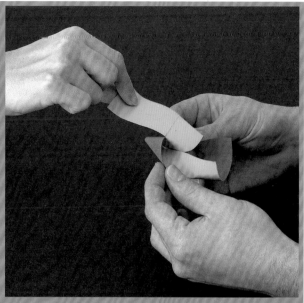

8. As you do this, the card will slowly begin to turn inside out. Do not rush this movement, or you may tear the card.

Secret View

9. Carefully pull the rolled edges all the way through the hole and open them out.

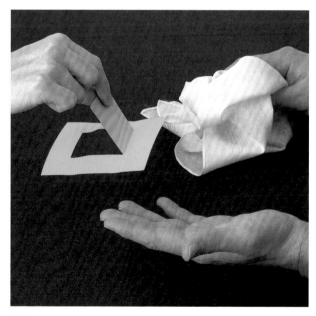

10. Now remove the handkerchief, and show that the card is now upside down!

Walking Through a Postcard

Give someone a postcard and a pair of scissors, and tell him it is possible to cut a hole in the card big enough for you to step through. See if he can figure out how. Unless he knows the secret, it is unlikely he will succeed.

1. Fold the postcard in half lengthwise. You can use a plain card or one with a picture on it.

2. Make straight cuts in from the folded edge approximately every ½ in (1 cm). Notice how each cut stops approximately ½ in (1 cm) short of the opposite edge.

3. Turn the card around, and cut more slits (marked here in red) between the slits you have already made, this time starting from the open edges rather than the fold. These slits stop ½ in (1 cm) from the folded edge, as before.

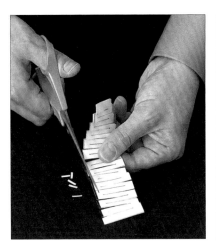

4. Now trim off about ⅛ in (3 mm) along the fold, except for the sections at each end.

5. When you open up the card, you will find it now has a hole in it large enough for you to step through.

6. If you want to show this stunt but don't have a postcard with you, you can use a business card or playing card instead, with the challenge: "Cut a hole big enough for me to put my head through."

A Cutting Problem

The solution to this simple puzzle requires a little lateral thinking, and the solution is guaranteed to make your audience groan. It would work very well as part of an act in conjunction with Suspended Animation, since both use the same props.

1. Tie a piece of string to the handle of a mug, and hold it up high. The challenge is to cut the string between the handle and your hand without the mug falling.

2. Tie a medium-size loop in the piece of string.

3. Snip through the loop, and the mug will stay where it is!

Quickness of the Hand

Have you heard the expression, "The quickness of the hand deceives the eye?" This little stunt proves the exact opposite. You see the money fall, but you can't close your hand fast enough. This surely proves the eye is quicker than the hand.

1. Hold a dollar bill at the very top, and ask someone to hold her finger and thumb open, ready to catch it. The idea is simple: You will drop the money and if she catches it, she can keep it! Don't worry: Your money is safe, as long as you make sure her fingers are open and halfway up the bill.

2. Her natural response will be too slow. The only way she will catch it is if she guesses when you are going to drop it.

Salt and Pepper Separation

How can you sort out a mixture of salt and pepper? This stunt makes use of static electricity to cause the particles of pepper to separate instantly from a pile of salt. This demonstrates once again how you can harness the laws of science to perform fun stunts.

1. Pour a quantity of salt onto a surface, which should preferably be dark so that you can see what is happening clearly.

2. Now sprinkle some ground pepper on top of the pile of salt on the paper.

3. Rub a balloon on your hair to create a static charge, and hold the balloon just above the pile of salt and pepper. The pepper will jump up and cling to the surface of the balloon while the salt stays on the table.

TIP

You can use a plastic comb instead of a balloon, if you prefer. Simply run the comb through your hair a few times, and then position the teeth close to the salt and pepper mixture. Try to use a white comb if you can, so that you can see the particles of pepper clearly.

Crazy Corks

You make a simple move with two corks and ask the spectators to copy you. While you can make the move with ease, they will get themselves in a tangle. The corks in the photographs have red dots on one end, and you should do the same to make the trick easy to follow.

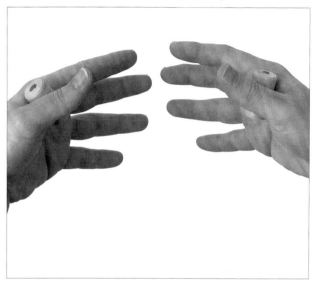

1. Pick up a cork in either hand, holding it in the crotch of the thumb as shown.

2. Turn your left wrist back toward you so that you can place the thumbs of both hands on the ends of the corks that do not have spots.

3. Now place the index finger of each hand on the ends of the corks that do have spots.

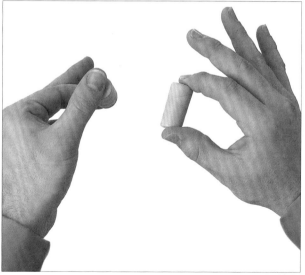

4. Untwist your left hand from your right, and the two corks will be separated. Of course, they were never really linked, but when others try to copy your moves they will find themselves in a state of confusion.

Interlocked

Two people have their wrists tied together with rope. The ropes are interlocked, and the challenge is for the two to separate without untying the knots. Unless they know the secret, this problem can take a long time to solve.

1. Tie a length of rope around both wrists of each of two people. Before you make the last knot, link the two ropes as shown.

2. To get free, one person must thread the center of his rope under the loop around one of the other person's wrists.

3. This loop is then slipped over the top of her hand.

4. The back view shows how the ropes are being untangled.

5. The result is that the two people have released one another without untying the knots.

Impossible Link

A pencil on a loop of string is attached to someone's buttonhole. While you seemed to put it on easily, he will have a tough time getting the pencil off again unless he knows the secret. This is a fantastic stunt to play on people, and is guaranteed to frustrate them.

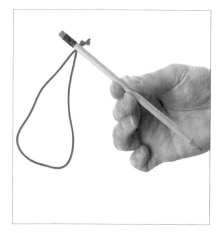

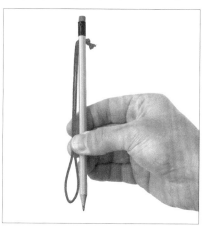

1. Pencils with string attached can sometimes be found in novelty and souvenir shops but are hard to find. It is easy to make your own by drilling a small hole in the top of a pencil and then tying a loop of string through the hole.

2. The loop of string must be a little shorter than the pencil (even when stretched to its full extent).

3. Pull a large section of the coat near a buttonhole through the loop of the string. You need to pull as much material through the loop as possible.

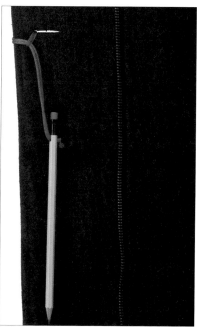

4. Carefully guide the tip of the pencil through the buttonhole of the coat. You may need to use a bit of force to get the angle right.

5. Gently pull the pencil through to complete the setup.

6. When your victim demands that you remove the pencil after failing miserably, do the following: Lift the pencil through the loop as far as it will go.

7. Pull the pencil out so that it is at a right angle to the buttonhole; then push the top back through the buttonhole.

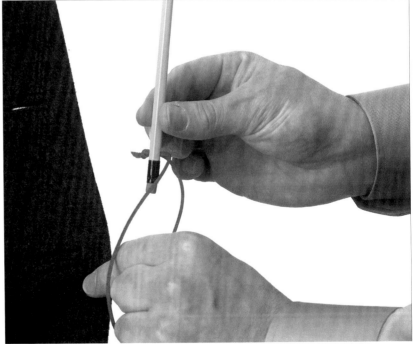

8. Hold on to the pencil, and once again pull as much fabric as you can through the loop of string.

9. You will now be able to remove the pencil completely.

Comedy Levitation

Your audience will gasp in amazement when they see you levitate your assistant – and laugh, too, if you show them how you did it. It is generally bad practice to expose a magic trick for the sake of a laugh, but this is more of a gag than a serious illusion.

1. To prepare the illusion, cut two full-size leg shapes out of an old cardboard box.

Secret View

2. Put a pair of your assistant's shoes on the ends of the fake legs and get her to hold the legs out in front of her, parallel to the ground. She will also need to lean her head back as far as possible to look as if she is lying down.

3. Cover your assistant in a sheet from the neck down. The sheet must cover the point where her feet touch the floor. The illusion of levitation is uncanny. You can either float your assistant across the stage and off the other side, or you can "accidentally" step on the sheet so that when your assistant moves across the stage, the cloth is pulled off to reveal the method.

=TIP=
Your assistant can be prepared offstage and float onto the stage at any point during your performance. If she bends her knees, and bobs up and down it will enhance the illusion of weightlessness.

Mini Me

This is another funny routine to use as part of a larger act. The curtains open, and there on the stage is a miniature, dancing, moving mini version of your assistant or yourself, depending on who is standing in front.

1. Stand in front of a table, and put your arms into a pair of trousers. The waistband should rest on your shoulders. Put your hands into a pair of shoes.

2. Now drape a jacket, back to front, around your shoulders.

Secret View

3. Have your assistant, who is kneeling behind you, put his arms through the arms of the jacket. From the front, he will remain unseen.

4. The two of you coordinate your movements, you can devise some really funny things for your Mini Me to do. Even simple things, like running your hands through your hair, look strange.

5. Try levitating off the table by simultaneously lifting the shoes up and fluttering your hands.

6. You can move from side to side and play with different objects. This is a lot of fun to try out.

Houdini Outdone!

Houdini was famous for escaping from locks, chains, prison cells and mailbags. In this version of one of his tricks, the escapologist is tied up inside a sack, but manages to escape in record time. This trick is incredibly simple to learn, as well as being a real showstopper.

1. You will need a sack large enough for your escapologist to climb into. If necessary, you can simply make your own from some cheap, porous, opaque fabric. There should be a number of holes around the top of the sack, through which you need to thread a rope.

Secret View

2. Leave some slack in the rope, and hide this extra length inside the sack.

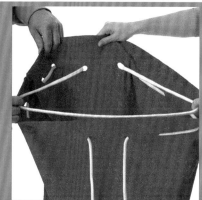

3. The extra loop should be equal to the circumference of the sack.

4. Prepare by arranging a screen on stage, and lay the sack out on the floor ready to step into.

5. The escapologist climbs into the sack and crouches down.

6. The assistant pulls the sack up over the escapologist's head.

7. This is what happens inside the sack: the escapologist steps on the extra loop of rope hidden inside.

8. The assistant pulls the rope ties the bag up. (The extra rope is still held under the escapologist's foot in the sack.)

9. Now the assistant places a screen in front of the sack and waits.

10. The escapologist releases the loop of rope and uses the slack to open the sack to escape.

11. After escaping, the escapologist reseals the sack by pulling on the rope.

12. The excess rope is then slipped back into the bag, leaving the knots in the front intact.

13. The escapologist walks in front of the screen holding the sack and receives the well-deserved applause.

Flip-Flap Production

Illusions don't have to be expensive to build. Here is a way to make someone appear using nothing more than a large cardboard carton. Now all you need to do is find a willing assistant and teach him or her how to perform this impressive trick.

1. Start with a tube of cardboard, simply made by cutting the top and bottom flaps off a large carton.

2. Tape a door to the front so that it swings freely in both directions.

3. Tape another door to the back, which should be hinged from the opposite side of the box.

4. Sit an assistant inside the box and close the doors. The illusion is ready.

5. Start the performance by opening the back door of the box.

Secret View

6. As you can see from this secret view, your assistant is inside but unseen by your audience.

Secret View

7. As you open the back door, the assistant crawls out of the box and behind the door, being very careful not to be seen.

8. When the front door is opened, the box looks perfectly empty. Remember, your assistant is completely hidden behind the back door.

9. Crouch down in the back so everyone can see you through the box.

10. Close the front door of the box. Your assistant now crawls back inside the box.

11. Close the back door, and make a magical gesture over the box.

12. Open the front door once again to reveal your assistant.

Bowl Vanish

Your assistant walks onto the stage carrying a big bowl on a tray. You show the audience a pitcher and pour its contents into the bowl. After covering the bowl with a large cloth, you lift it off the tray and walk to the front of the stage. On a count of three, you throw the cloth into the air with a flourish: The bowl of liquid vanishes completely! This clever illusion has been used by many of the world's greatest magicians. Although you need to prepare several gimmicks, they are easy to make, and the illusion is not too difficult to perform. Its success depends on how well you make the props and how much you rehearse with your assistant. Teamwork is the key word here. Although your assistant doesn't seem to do much, in reality he or she does most of the work while you take all the credit.

1. Trace the top of the bowl you are using, and then cut out a disc of thick cardboard just a tiny bit larger – 1/8 in (3 mm) all around.

2. This "form" needs to be attached to the center of a large square of cloth. You can do this using double-sided adhesive tape. Attach a second identical cloth, so that the cardboard form is sandwiched between the layers. You can stitch around the edges, but it is easier and quicker to use iron-on bonding fabric or fusible web.

3. Fold the cloth neatly around the form so that it cannot be seen, and place the cloth to one side while you prepare the other props.

4. Cut out the absorbent section of a disposable diaper. This contains crystals that can absorb many times their own weight in water.

5. Use double-sided adhesive tape to secure the diaper inside the bowl. Push it down well below the rim so that it will not be seen.

6. Apply a big ball of reusable putty adhesive to the underside of the bowl.

7. Position the bowl in the center of a tray, pressing it down firmly to make sure it is securely attached.

8. To complete the setup, place a pitcher of liquid and the prepared cloth on the tray beside the bowl.

9. In performance, your assistant walks on stage carrying the tray. It is important that no one can see the diaper inside the bowl.

10. You take the pitcher of liquid, hold it in the air, and slowly pour it into the bowl. Unknown to your audience, the liquid is being absorbed by the diaper.

11. Give the pitcher to your assistant, who holds it in one hand while holding the tray with the other. Pick up the cloth, flick it open, and display it front and back.

12. Cover the bowl so that the cardboard form sits precisely on top of it. You must practice this move so that it happens smoothly and without hesitation.

13. Hold onto the form between both hands as your assistant lowers the tray. The tray is allowed to fall with its underside to the audience. The bowl, with the soaked diaper inside, is safely attached and hidden by the tray.

14. Your assistant now walks offstage holding the tray and the pitcher while you walk forward, supposedly holding the bowl between your hands. Mime this so that it looks as though the bowl has some weight.

15. Get ready to throw the cloth in the air. Count to three.

16. On "three," toss the cloth high into the air.

17. Aim to catch the cloth by the corners as it comes back down, and flick it out a few times, turning it from back to front to show that it is truly empty.

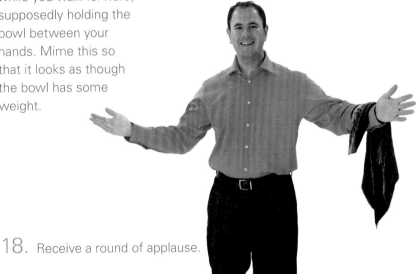

18. Receive a round of applause.

TIP
This is the cheapest way to make the props, but of course you can make a more professional job of it. For instance, you can attach the bowl permanently to the tray, rather than using adhesive putty.

Victory Cartons Illusion

In the mid-1900s a magician named U.F. Grant created many illusions that could be performed using props made of cardboard cartons. One of his most successful ideas was this one, which is used by professional magicians to this day. It is a great illusion, and you should practice hard to do it justice. You will find that the boxes last longer if you reinforce the edges with brown tape.

1. Cut the top and bottom flaps off a large carton, or make one to the exact size you need from four separate pieces of double-walled corrugated cardboard taped together.

2. Now find or make a second carton, which should be about 1 in (2.5 cm) taller than the first. Cut off the top and bottom flaps of this too, and cut a large hole in one side, leaving a border of approximately 3 in (7.5 cm) all around.

3. Flatten the cartons and set them down, as shown here. The box with the hole goes in the front, with the hole concealed in the back.

Secret View

4. Your assistant is hiding unseen behind the back box.

5. Pick up the front box. This is the one with a hole in one panel, so be careful not to let it show.

6. Open it out and place it next to you. Notice how the box overlaps the one behind it.

7. As you position this box your assistant sneaks carefully inside, keeping low and entering the box as quickly and quietly as possible. If you are busy positioning the box at the same time, any extra movement of the box as the assistant enters will be unnoticed.

8. Pick up the remaining box, open it and hold it up high to show the audience that it is empty.

9. This is how things look from the back at this stage.

10. Place this second box over the first. Once you have done this, you can even spin both boxes around, as long as you are careful not to lift them off the ground.

11. Finally, make a magical gesture and your assistant pops up into view.

Cutting a Person in Two

One of the most famous illusions of all time is Sawing a Lady in Half. The first version was invented by P.T. Selbit, and it was first performed in the early 1920s. In this version, two ropes pass through the middle of a volunteer from the audience.

1. Prepare two 6 ft (2 m) lengths of rope by loosely tying them together in the center with a loop of cotton thread.

2. Invite an audience member onto the stage to be your assistant. Give him or her one end of the two ropes while you hold the other and tug them to prove their solidity.

Secret View

3. Invite another audience member onto the stage. As he or she approaches, readjust the ropes in your hand by exchanging the ends so that you hold the centers of both, and they are looped back on themselves but held together by the thread.

4. Pass the prepared rope behind the volunteer, and hand the ends to your helper. This secret view from the back clearly shows what is really happening with the ropes.

5. Bring one rope from either side in front of the volunteer, and tie a single overhand knot, apparently making things even more secure.

Secret View

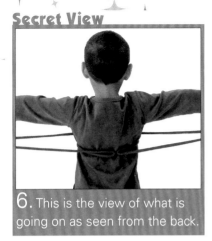

6. This is the view of what is going on as seen from the back.

7. On a count of three, pull the ropes. The thread will snap, and it will seem as if the ropes have passed right through your volunteer's body. (The reason this works is that you switch the ends in step 3 and then switch them back again by tying the knot in step 5.)

Metamorphosis

This is another of the most famous illusions in the world. This simple version is a very serviceable alternative for the aspiring amateur illusionist. Like the Victory Cartons Illusion, it was introduced to the magical fraternity by U.F. Grant. Make sure that you work against a dark backdrop to avoid light spilling through the back of the box and showing through the front air holes.

1. You will need a cardboard box big enough for you to get inside. Cut out eight air holes, four in the front and four in the back. Show the box to your audience.

2. Your assistant steps into the box. The assistant must be equipped with a retractable craft knife in his or her pocket.

3. Close the lid of the box, and start sealing it up with packing tape, explaining what you are doing to the audience.

Secret View

4. While you are sealing the top of the box, your assistant cuts through the back panel, cutting between the air holes. The noise of the tape being applied and you talking to the audience will cover the noise of your assistant cutting.

Secret View

5. Arrange a screen in front of the box. From behind, you can see that the hole has already been cut along three edges in the back by the assistant inside the box.

6. Stand in front of the screen and tell your audience to watch carefully. Talking will give your assistant more time, and it will also help to cover any noises he or she may inadvertently make.

Secret View

7. After about 30 seconds, walk behind the screen.

8. As you do so, your assistant should be crawling out of the box.

9. Without hesitation, the assistant walks around to the front of the screen as you crawl into the box.

10. The screen is immediately pushed to one side, and your assistant starts to pull the tape off the box.

11. As the lid opens, you stand up in the box to prove that you changed places in a split second.

Tip Over Box

This illusion is also used by magicians the world over and is incredibly deceptive. A cardboard box is shown to be empty, but the top bursts open and the magician's assistant jumps out. You can make this style of box any size and use it to make any object appear.

1. Cut off the top and bottom flaps of a large carton if you have one, or make your own in the size you need by taping four sheets of double-walled corrugated cardboard together.

2. Cut a cardboard panel to act as a lid, and tape it on so that it will open and close with ease.

3. Cut another cardboard panel, and tape it to the bottom. It is hinged along the edge that is diagonally opposite the hinge of the lid to form a flap that folds inward.

4. Tape a strip of cardboard along the bottom edge, opposite the hinge of the flap, as shown here.

5. Securely fasten a handle to the flap using tape, so that it will be on the inside of the box, and the box is ready.

Secret View

6. To perform the illusion, have your assistant already inside the box, with the secret flap folded up inside it.

7. Tip the box forward until the front panel reaches the floor. Your assistant stays still and holds onto the handle on the flap. The lower front edge does not move at any time.

8. From the front, no one can see that your assistant is now behind the box.

9. Open the lid, which is now in the front, so that the audience can see that the box is empty.

Secret View

10. This is the view of what is happening from the back.

11. Close the lid, and tip the box upright again. Your assistant will now be back inside the box.

12. Open the lid of the box at the top, and build the suspense.

13. Your assistant makes his big entrance by jumping up and out of the box.

Out of Thin Air

If you want to make an impact at the start of your show, this is a great way to achieve it. You show a large cloth, and with a shake, your assistant appears underneath. The whole illusion takes only seconds to perform, but the element of surprise makes it very impressive. No one is expecting a person to appear. This trick will work with any large prop, as long as it completely hides your assistant.

Secret View

1. Your assistant will need to hide behind a large prop covered with a cloth. If your act includes any of the illusions in this chapter that utilize a carton, that would work well.

2. Say to the audience, "I bet you're wondering what's underneath this cloth."

Secret View

3. Pull the cloth off the prop with both hands, and bring it in front of you. Position yourself so that the edge of the cloth just overlaps the edge of the box when viewed from the front. Your assistant quickly and silently crawls behind the cloth. Continue your patter, saying, "It's a box."

4. Now you raise the cloth and as you do so, your assistant stands behind it.

5. This is how it looks from behind. Raise the cloth only for an instant: the faster you can make the raising and lowering of the cloth, the better this illusion will look.

6. Lower the cloth with a magical flourish and say: "And this is my lovely assistant!"

Inverted Glass Trick

In another funny stunt, you turn a glass of liquid upside down, without the liquid leaking out. It is now impossible to turn the glass the right way without the liquid spilling and making a mess. Only perform this stunt on a suitable surface.

1. Cover a glass of liquid with a piece of card stock. Here, we have used colored liquid so you can see what is happening, but it can be anything.

2. Quickly turn everything upside down, holding the card firmly against the mouth of the glass to keep any of the liquid from escaping.

3. Place the glass and the card upside down on a table.

4. Slide out the card and the glass will remain full, but upside down. It is now impossible to move the glass without creating a complete mess, so don't try this in the dining room or in someone else's home without permission.

confederate An accomplice in a magic performance; stooge.

conundrum A riddle or brainteaser.

disassemble To take apart.

dissipate To spread thin and scatter in different directions; disperse.

escapologist A magician who specializes in escaping from ropes, handcuffs, boxes and other traps; an escape artist.

feat An act of skill, strength, daring or imagination; an achievement.

gag A practical joke.

gimmick An object that has been altered to help produce a magical effect.

hypnosis A sleeplike trance state, in which one is thought to be more receptive to suggestion and direction.

hypnotize To influence or overcome with the power of suggestion; to put into a state of hypnosis.

illusion A large-scale magic trick designed for a large audience, often involving people, animals or other large items.

illusionist A magician who performs illusions, such as sawing a person in half or levitating a person.

involuntarily Done without one's choice or conscious control.

levitation The ability to make an object or person float in the air with no visible means of support.

mime To imitate.

opaque Not allowing light to pass through.

porous Allowing gases and liquids, like air and water, to pass through.

predicament A difficult, puzzling or unpleasant situation.

stooge Audience member who is planted as part of the act.

stunt A feat displaying unusual skill, strength or courage, often performed to attract attention.

American Museum of Magic

107 East Michigan Avenue
Marshall, MI 49068
(269) 781-7570
Web site: http://www.americanmuseumofmagic.org
The American Museum of Magic has a collection of nearly one million magic artifacts, including props, costumes, lithographs, posters, photographs and other memorabilia. The museum's Lund Memorial Library contains about 15,000 books and thousands of magic periodicals.

History Museum at the Castle

330 East College Avenue
Appleton, WI 54911
(920) 735-9370
Web site: http://www.foxvalleyhistory.org
This local history museum contains an exhibit called A.K.A. Houdini, which displays and interprets information related to the great magician Harry Houdini. The online companion exhibit is a rich resource for learning about the man's life and work.

International Brotherhood of Magicians (IBM)

13 Point West Boulevard
St. Charles, MO 63301-4431
(636) 724-2400
Web site: http://www.magician.org
The International Brotherhood of Magicians (IBM) is a well-respected magic organization with over three hundred local rings, or chapters, worldwide. The organization welcomes amateur and professional magicians, magic collectors and people with an interest in the art of magic.

Magicana

15 Madison Avenue
Toronto, ON M5R 2S2
Canada
(416) 913-9034
Web site: http://www.magicana.com
Magicana is a charitable arts organization dedicated to advancing magic as a performing art. Its outreach programs for children and seniors employ magic as a teaching vehicle in the community. The organization has a wide range of resources, including a magic collection, classes and seminars, publications and blogs.

Magic Castle Junior Society

7001 Franklin Avenue

Hollywood, CA 90028-8600

(323) 851-3313

Web site: http://www.magiccastle.com/juniors

Teens with a serious interest in magic can apply to the junior society of the Magic Castle, a prestigious private magic club in Hollywood. After passing an audition for acceptance, members develop their magical interests through workshops, networking, and exposure to leading professional magicians.

Society of American Magicians (SAM)

Society of Young Magicians (SYM)

P.O. Box 2900

Pahrump, NV 89041

(702) 610-1050

Web sites: http://www.magicsam.com; http://www.magicsym.com

Founded in 1902, the Society of American Magicians (SAM) is a worldwide organization dedicated to the art of magic. The Society of Young Magicians (SYM) is its youth branch, serving people ages 7–17 who are interested in learning and performing magic. SYM has about sixty local assemblies, or chapters, around the world, including in Canada, South Africa and Bermuda.

Web Sites

Due to the changing nature of Internet links, Rosen Publishing has developed an online list of Web sites related to the subject of this book. This site is updated regularly. Please use this link to access the list:

http://www.rosenlinks.com/mag/stun

Barnhart, Norm. *Amazing Magic Tricks: Expert Level* (Edge Books: Magic Tricks). Mankato, MN: Capstone Press, 2009.

Bednar, Chuck. *David Blaine: Illusionist and Endurance Artist* (Transcending Race in America). Broomall, PA: Mason Crest Publishers, 2010.

Carlson, Laurie M. *Harry Houdini for Kids: His Life and Adventures with 21 Magic Tricks and Illusions*. Chicago, IL: Chicago Review Press, 2009.

Cobb, Vicki. *On Stage* (Where's the Science Here?). Minneapolis, MN: Millbrook Press, 2006.

Fleischman, Sid. *Escape! The Story of the Great Houdini*. New York, NY: Greenwillow Books, 2006.

Kaufman, Richard. *Knack Magic Tricks: A Step-by-Step Guide to Illusions, Sleights of Hand, and Amazing Feats*. Guilford, CT: Knack, 2010.

Keable-Elliott, Ian. *The Big Book of Magic Fun*. Hauppage, NY: Barrons Educational Series, Inc., 2005.

Kieve, Paul. *Hocus Pocus: A Tale of Magnificent Magicians*. New York, NY: Scholastic, 2008.

Krull, Kathleen. *Houdini: World's Greatest Mystery Man and Escape King*. New York, NY: Walker & Co., 2005.

Longe, Bob. *No Boredom Allowed! Nutty Challenges & Zany Dares*. New York, NY: Sterling, 2008.

Mason, Tom. *Magic of the Masters: Learn Tricks by David Copperfield, Harry Houdini and More!* (Top Secret Magic). New York, NY: Scholastic, 2007.

Mullin, Rita T. *Harry Houdini: Death-Defying Showman* (Sterling Biographies). New York, NY: Sterling, 2007.

Mundi, Mariah. *The Midas Box*. London, UK: Faber and Faber, 2007.

Price, Sean. *Vanished! Magic Tricks and Great Escapes* (Culture in Action). Chicago, IL: Raintree, 2010.

Schendlinger, Mary. *Prepare to Be Amazed*. Toronto, Canada: Annick Press, 2005.

Selznick, Brian. *The Houdini Box*. New York, NY: Atheneum Books for Young Readers, 2008.

Steinmeyer, Jim. *Hiding the Elephant: How Magicians Invented the Impossible and Learned to Disappear*. New York, NY: Carroll & Graf Publishers, 2004.

Tremaine, Jon. *Instant Magic*. Hauppauge, NY: Barrons, 2009.

Zenon, Paul. *Magic of the Mind: Tricks for the Master Magician* (Amazing Magic). Rosen Central, 2008.

INDEX

About the Author

Nicholas Einhorn is a Gold Star member of the Inner Magic Circle. He has won a number of industry awards for his work including: The Magic Circle Centenary Close-Up Magician 2005; F.I.S.M (World Magic Championships) Award Winner 2003; The Magic Circle Close-Up Magician of the Year 2002; and The Magic Circle Close-Up Magician of the Year 1996. Einhorn uses his magic to build crowds for some of the world's largest companies at business trade shows and exhibitions. He has many TV credits to his name and is regularly invited to lecture at magic societies and conventions around the globe. As a magic consultant, Einhorn has designed and created the special effects for several large-scale stage productions, as well as consulted on the film *Bright Young Things*, directed by Stephen Fry. He also develops and markets new magic effects for the magic fraternity. His illusions have been purchased and performed by magicians all over the world, including some of the biggest names in magic, such as Paul Daniels and David Copperfield.